Hello, Family Members,

Learning to read is one of the most importa[...] of early childhood. **Hello Reader!** books are [...] children become skilled readers who like to read. Beginning readers learn to read by remembering frequently used words like "the," "is," and "and"; by using phonics skills to decode new words; and by interpreting picture and text clues. These books provide both the stories children enjoy and the structure they need to read fluently and independently. Here are suggestions for helping your child *before, during,* and *after* reading:

Before

• Look at the cover and pictures and have your child predict what the story is about.
• Read the story to your child.
• Encourage your child to chime in with familiar words and phrases.
• Echo read with your child by reading a line first and having your child read it after you do.

During

• Have your child think about a word he or she does not recognize right away. Provide hints such as "Let's see if we know the sounds" and "Have we read other words like this one?"
• Encourage your child to use phonics skills to sound out new words.
• Provide the word for your child when more assistance is needed so that he or she does not struggle and the experience of reading with you is a positive one.
• Encourage your child to have fun by reading with a lot of expression . . . like an actor!

After

• Have your child keep lists of interesting and favorite words.
• Encourage your child to read the books over and over again. Have him or her read to brothers, sisters, grandparents, and even teddy bears. Repeated readings develop confidence in young readers.
• Talk about the stories. Ask and answer questions. Share ideas about the funniest and most interesting characters and events in the stories.

I do hope that you and your child enjoy this book.

— Francie Alexander
   Reading Specialist,
   Scholastic's Learning Ventures

For Sophia Flynt Kriegel,
who *loves* bugs.
— M.B.

Special thanks to Laurie Roulston
of the Denver Museum of Natural History
for her expertise

Text copyright © 2000 by Melvin Berger.

Photography credits:

Cover: Brian Kenney; page 6 (magnifying glass): Ana Esperanza Nance; page 6 (inset of mosquito): Rod Planck/Photo Researchers; page 8: E.R. Degginger/Dembinsky Photo Associates; page 9: Robert and Linda Mitchell; page 10 (upper): Robert and Linda Mitchell; page 10 (lower): Brian Kenney; page 11: Robert and Linda Mitchell; page 13: Brian Kenney; page 15 (magnifying glass): Ana Esperanza Nance; page 15 (inset of monarch butterfly egg): E.R. Degginger/Photo Researchers; pages 16-17: Harry Rogers/Photo Researchers; page 18 (left): E.R. Degginger/Photo Researchers; page 18 (right) and page 19 (left): John Mitchell/Photo Researchers; page 19 (right): Michael Lustbader/Photo Researchers; page 20 (left): Brian Kenney; page 20 (right): M.H. Sharp/Photo Researchers; page 21 (upper): John Bova/Photo Researchers; page 21 (lower): Dan Demspter/Dembinsky Photo Associates; page 22: Skip Moody/Dembinsky Photo Associates; page 24: Robert and Linda Mitchell; page 25: Dan Guravich/Photo Researchers; page 26: Scott Camazine/Photo Researchers; page 27: J.H. Robinson/Photo Researchers; page 28: Robert and Linda Mitchell; page 29: Charles R. Belinky/Photo Researchers; pages 30-32: Robert and Linda Mitchell; page 33: Harry Rogers/Photo Researchers; page 34: Jerome Wexler/Photo Researchers; page 36: R. J. Erwin/Photo Researchers; page 37 (upper): Robert and Linda Mitchell; page 38: Robert and Linda Mitchell; page 39: Jim W. Grace/Photo Researchers; page 40 (lower left): Dan Guravich/Photo Researchers; page 40 (right): Gary Retherford/Photo Researchers.

Library of Congress Cataloging-in-Publication Data

Berger, Melvin.
　　Buzz! : a book about insects / by Melvin Berger.
　　　　p.　　cm. — (Hello reader! Science. Level 3)
　　　　Summary: Presents information about a variety of insects, including flies, bees, butter-
　　flies, and caterpillars.
　　　　ISBN: 0-439-08748-1
　　　　1. Insects —Juvenile literature.　　[1. Insects.]　　I. Title. II. Series.
　　QL467.2.B47　　2000
　　595.7—dc21　　　　　　　　　　　　　　　　　　　　　99-041768

12 11 10 9 8 7 6 5 4 3 2 1　　　　　　　　　　00 01 02 03 04 05 06

Printed in the U.S.A.
First printing, May 2000

23

BUZZ!

A Book About Insects

by Melvin Berger

Hello Reader! Science — Level 3

SCHOLASTIC INC. Cartwheel B·O·O·K·S®
New York Toronto London Auckland Sydney
Mexico City New Delhi Hong Kong

CHAPTER 1
Insects and You

It's a warm summer day.

You're at a picnic.

Everything is ready.

BUZZ!

Flies land on the bread.

Shoo, flies!

BUZZ!

Bees buzz around the juice.

Away, bees!

Flies and bees are insects.

So are mosquitoes and ants, wasps
and butterflies, ladybugs and fireflies.
Caterpillars and grasshoppers, moths
and dragonflies, crickets and termites
are insects, too.

Insects are all around.
Wherever you go, you find them.
And they find you!

All in all, there are about one million
different kinds of insects.
And there are billions of each kind.

Insects are special in a few ways.
Most have wings. And all

- are tiny,

- need little food,

- can live almost anywhere,

- have six legs,

- have two long feelers or antennae
  (an-TEN-ee).

Insects see.

They have two huge eyes.

Each eye is like many tiny eyes.

They let insects see to the front, back, and sides.

Insects hear — but they don't have ears.
Crickets hear with spots on their
front legs.
Caterpillars hear through hairs
on their body.
Moths have "eardrums" on their sides.

Insects smell — but not with noses.
They use their antennae.
Have you ever seen
an ant waving
its antennae?
It is picking
up smells in
the air.

Insects breathe — but not with lungs.
Most have holes along their sides.
They usually breathe in through
the front holes.
And breathe out through the
back ones.

Insects taste — but not with tongues.
Flies, bees, and butterflies taste with
their feet.
Ants and wasps taste with their
antennae.

Insects eat — but in various ways.

Take dung beetles, for example.

They roll up balls of manure to feed their young.

Flies spit on their food.

The spit turns solid food into mush.

Then the fly soaks up its meal.

Insects can't talk, of course.
Yet many make sounds.
Crickets rub their wings together.
Moths blow air out of their mouths.
Termites tap with their heads.

Insects may be pests at picnics.
But aren't they amazing?

CHAPTER 2
How Insects Are Born

Insects are born from eggs.

The eggs are smaller than grains
of rice.

Female insects lay eggs
in different places.

Butterflies lay eggs on plant leaves.

Flies lay eggs on rotten food.

Mosquitoes lay eggs on water.

In time the eggs hatch.

But what's this?
The newborns don't look like
their parents!
Each looks like a small worm.
It is called a larva.

The larva has only
one thing to do.
Eat, eat, eat, eat!
It grows bigger and bigger.
Soon it is too big for its hard skin.
The larva wiggles out — and grows a
new skin!

The larva sheds its skin
up to 12 times.
Then it stops eating.
It makes a cover around itself.
Now it is a pupa (PYOO-puh).

Inside, the
pupa changes
into an adult.
Flies change in a few days.
Some butterflies take several months.
Out comes a full-grown, adult insect.

Egg, larva, pupa, adult.

Most insects go through these four changes.

Yet not all do.

A few insect eggs hatch in a different way.

What's this?

These newborns *do* look like their parents!

They differ in only three ways.

They're smaller, another color, and

have no wings.

Each newborn is called

a nymph.

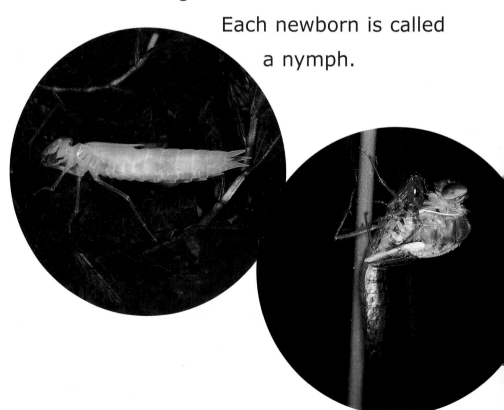

The nymph eats and grows.
It sheds its outer shell again and again.
Each time, the wings get bigger.
Finally, the nymph becomes an adult.

Egg, nymph, adult.
Only a few insects go through these
three stages.
Among them are crickets, grasshoppers,
mayflies, roaches, and dragonflies.

Most female insects lay hundreds of eggs.
Some lay millions or billions.
Why so many?

Insects face lots of dangers.
Birds, frogs, bears, and many other animals
gobble them up.
Other insects attack them.
And humans kill them.
Insects must lay huge numbers of eggs.
If not, they will die out.

Insects also defend themselves.
Some fly, jump, or run away
from their enemies.
Others are hard to spot.
Green caterpillars look like leaves.
Gray moths look like
tree bark.
Walkingstick
insects look like
twigs.

Some insects fight back.

A few kinds of beetles squirt poison.

Ants bite.

And stink bugs just smell bad!

What about insects with bright colors?

Most of them have stingers or poisons.

Animals learn to leave these insects alone.

Many billions of insects are born.

Large numbers die.

Still, billions live on.

CHAPTER 3
Insects in Winter

Do you wonder where insects go
in winter?
Many don't go anywhere.
They lay eggs and die.

Take crickets, for example.
They lay their eggs in the ground.
Then the adults die.
In spring, the eggs hatch.
Out come the cricket nymphs.

Some insects migrate (MY-grate) in winter.
They leave their homes and travel to
other places.
They go where the weather is warm and
there is plenty to eat.
There they stay until spring.
Then they come home.

Monarch butterflies migrate.
Every fall, they fly south.
Some fly more
than 2,000 miles
to Mexico.
No insects
migrate farther
than monarchs.

In spring, the monarchs start for home.
Along the way the females lay eggs.
The adults die.
But the eggs hatch.

Other insects hibernate (HY-bur-nate)
in winter.
They go to sleep in places that are warm
and safe.

Flies, ladybugs, and mosquitoes hibernate.
They sleep all winter inside attics, cellars,
and caves.

Honeybees hide inside hives in winter.

The bees pile up in one big ball.

They eat the honey they made during the summer.

On warm days, some fly out to find more food.

Ants hide in nests in the ground.
Each nest has many rooms.
In winter, the ants live in the
deepest rooms.
They eat food that they have stored.

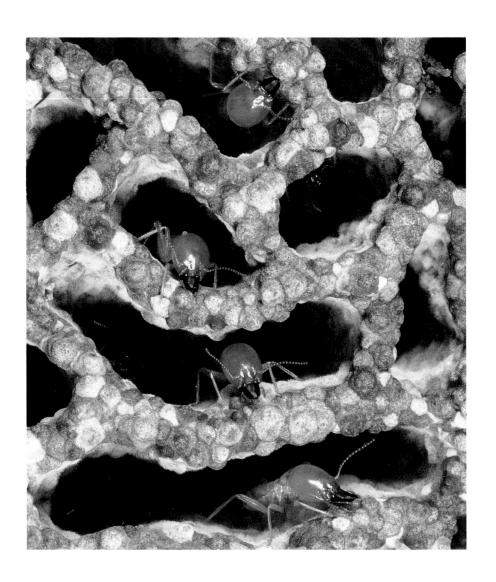

Caterpillars make covers around
themselves.
We call them cocoons.
The cocoons hang from branches.
The caterpillars stay warm and dry inside.
In spring, they come out as butterflies.

So what do insects do in winter?
Many die.
Others travel, sleep, or hide
and wait for spring.

CHAPTER 4
Insects At Home

Most insects live alone.
But some live in huge colonies.

A colony can have thousands of insects.
Usually the biggest insect is the queen.
Most colonies have only one queen.

The queen's main job is to lay eggs.
She can lay as many as 2,000 eggs
a day!

Most of the other insects in the colony are workers.

They are usually female and they have important jobs.

The workers take care of the young.

They protect the colony.

They find food for all the bees in the hive.

And they clean the nest.

Each colony also has a few hundred males.

Their job is to mate with the queen.

Then they die.

Honeybees live in colonies.

Their home is usually a hive inside a box
or hollow tree.

Workers build the hive with wax they
make themselves.

Each hive has many tiny cells.

Here the workers raise the young
and store food.

In warm weather the workers flit
from flower to flower.
They suck up a liquid called nectar.
And they gather a powder called pollen.

Honeybee workers carry the nectar
and pollen back to the hive.
They eat the pollen.
And they change the nectar into honey.
Some of the honey they eat.
The rest they store in the hive.

A female honeybee can sting.
The stinger is at the end of her body.
Sometimes a honeybee
stings an animal or
person.
It cannot pull out
the stinger.
So the bee flies
off without it.

Certain ants also sting.

The fire ant is the worst.

It locks its jaws in another insect's flesh.

Then it lowers its back end and OUCH! —
it stings.

Ants usually build their colonies
in the soil.

Worker ants dig tunnels in the earth.

Ants mostly eat fruit and nectar.
They carry the food back to the colony.
As they go, they press their bodies
to the ground.
This leaves a smell trail that other ants
follow to get more food.

Harvester ants
gather seeds.
They chew them
into a food called
"ant bread."

Some ants capture tiny insects
called aphids.
They have a good reason.
Aphids suck plant juices.
The aphids turn the juices into a sweet
liquid called honeydew.

The ants stroke the aphids with
their antennae.
This makes the aphids give up drops
of honeydew.
The ants just lap it up.